Book Description

Are you interested in maximizing your energy   to find
a natural way to alleviate the symptoms of your disease? Do you wish
for days when your mind, emotions and physical body can be
perfectly in sync? If you answer yes to these questions, then this is
the right book for you.

Chakras for Beginners is a book that focuses on how you can use
chakras to find balance in your life. Chakras are basically energy
centers in your body, and there are seven main energy centers. These
centers can all be easily traced using your spine. Understanding these
centers, and how they move in and affect your life, can help you find
healing for a variety of physical, mental and emotional issues you may
be facing. These issues include addiction, stress, and lack of
confidence, self-awareness, obesity and more. The energy centers that
chakras represent can be found on your lower back, all the way to the
top of your head. For ease of differentiation, each chakra is
represented with a name and a color.

These centers of energy can affect not only your mood, but your
ability to execute day to day tasks. They can be stimulated on a daily
basis, so that you can live your life at the fullest peace and well-being,
using the energy that is within you. The challenge comes in when you
begin to consider how they should be used. Using your chakras
involves becoming aware of them, and thinking of ways that they can
be used to promote health and balance.

Whenever you are focusing on your chakras, you may find that they
are in perfect balance or a state of imbalance, although an imbalance
is more likely. It is best to try and feel through all of them, so that
you can identify the one that you need to work on the most. If you
can identify what is causing you the imbalance, you can then take up
the opportunity to use healing exercises to create a balance.

A block or imbalance in chakras will lead to the slowing down of a basic life force. This can negatively affect every area of your life, leading to physical pain, mental anguish or emotional misery. As this affects the person's mood, you may appear to be tired, depressed or listless. If your chakras are balanced, you promote health and well-being.

This book contains details of exercises that you can conduct to help you understand the basics of chakras and how you can apply them to your life.

To explain the healing and balancing power of chakras, this book is divided into seven chapters. Each chapter addresses a particular chakra. They include:

1) Root Chakra
2) Sacral / Naval Chakra
3) Solar Plexus Chakra
4) Heart Chakra
5) Throat Chakra
6) Third Eye / Brow Chakra
7) Crown Chakra

To begin your restoration of energy journey, read on for tips, additional factors, strategies, healing methodologies and detailed explanations on the seven different chakras.

CHAKRAS FOR BEGINNERS:

Discover the seven major chakras, how to balance your chakras and how balancing your chakras will help you with healing emotional, physical and mental imbalances

ALICIA STEVENS

Introduction

With all the activities and interactions you may face in the day, it becomes difficult for you to fully experience being balanced and peaceful. When you are imbalanced, your energy is unable to flow freely and you may feel mentally unable to process your thoughts, emotionally out of whack, difficulty communicating, and physically exhausted to the point that you are not motivated to do any activity. The worst case scenario in being imbalanced is the effect it can have on your health, causing an increase in the illnesses you could suffer from.

To bring your entire mind and body back to balance, you can improve the flow of energy to the body using the seven chakras. The word chakra is derived from Sanskrit and it means wheel. Chakras are visualized as wheels of energy that are continuously rotating within your body. They each rotate at a different speed, with the first chakra mobbing at the slowest speed, and the seventh chakra moving at the highest speed.

There are many ways to interpret and understand the way that chakras can be used for healing and finding balance. By breaking down some of the different ways they work, you can start to understand what you can do with the chakras in your body. The most popular methods are meditation, sound, yoga and visualization. However, these methods cannot be replicated for each and every chakra, as some chakras focus on the mind, while others focus on the body and its well-being.

The seven chakras tie in with your zodiac sign, helping you to determine which chakra is your main source of power; therefore, the one that may need the most balance or healing. In addition, understanding the power of gemstones and crystals on your chakras will help with your clearing, revitalizing and healing activities of your body and soul.

Crystals and gemstones are excellent healing tools, as they have a piezoelectric effect. They are able to respond to the electricity going through your body, help balance and stimulate your energy, as well as, harmonize them.

This book contains the different ways that you can maximize the energy from your chakras.

CHAPTER 1 – The Root Chakra

"Others show you yourself and what you need to work on within, by their reflection of your own rejected or denied emotions."

This chakra is also known as *Muladhava* in Sanskrit.

This is the first chakra, and it is focused on the lower body. It is one of three chakras that works with the physical aspect of the body. The root chakra represents your foundation and feeling of being grounded. The energy center is located at the base of the spine in the tailbone area. The root chakra can help with your emotional issues, particularly those that center on your financial independence, self preservation, money, personal survival and food. It stands for your inherited beliefs through your formative years.

In fact, events that take place in your life between the ages of 0-7 can have a very strong effect on your root chakra and sense of balance. If you did not experience an adequate amount of love in these years, then you will experience anxiety, restlessness and emotional dysfunction often. It is during these early years that the foundation is set for building relationships with parents, siblings and the community.

When you are practicing healing exercises for the root chakra, it is important to note that it is about feeling grounded. A basic exercise that you can do to feel grounded is stomping the ground with your bare feet. If you would like to accomplish long term healing using the root chakra, then you need to work on some physical activities, as this chakra focuses on the physical part of the chakras. In addition to physical activity, smell oriented treatments have been proven to be effective, as well as the use of gemstones which come from the earth and are meant to improve on your energy center. You can also tap into the healing power of this chakra from the food you consume. Food such as beetroot and apples are red in color, like the color that represents this chakra. Other foods that can be used for healing include hot spices like Tabasco, cayenne peppers and red meat.

When the root chakra is healthy, it connects you with vitality to your family of origin, immediate society and global community.

The root chakra is the starting point when you are looking to study individual chakras. This energy center focuses on the basic needs for survival, safety and security. It is related to the Earth mother, who provides use the ability of being grounded. If you are looking to accomplish anything in the material world, or to gain any possessions, you will need the energy for success from the chakra.

The problems associated with an imbalance in root chakra include obesity, anorexia nervosa and knee troubles. The root chakra governs lower body parts such as the hips, legs, lower back and sexual organs, particularly those of males.

This chakra is represented by the color red. The color red represents self- awareness. This area focuses on survival and stability, and the reason you are here on this earth. The color red provides power from the earth, while giving energy on all levels. As much as this color has positive sides, there is also a negative angle to the color red. Should your chakra be unbalanced for any reason, those with a bright root chakra are likely to feel tearful, insecure, aggressive or fearful.

If you wish to connect to healing using a gemstone for the first chakra, then you should consider the Smokey Quartz, Obsidian, Black Tourmaline or Garret.

CHAPTER 2 – Sacral/Naval Chakra

"Emotional addictions are felt, accepted, loved and forgiven."

The Sanskrit name for this chakra is *Svadhisthana*.

This is the second chakra in the sequence of seven. The sacral chakra governs the zodiac signs of Pisces, Cancer and Scorpio. This shows that the sacral chakra is related to the water element. Therefore, if you belong to one of these signs, then it is quite likely that this chakra is the brightest and perhaps even the most active chakra on your body. On the human body, this chakra is the second from the bottom of the seven chakras. The energy center is located within the lower abdomen, approximately two inches under the naval and two inches in; and is rooted in the spine. It is worth noting that this chakra affects the emotional sexuality of women, whereas the root chakra affects the general (mainly physical) sexuality of men. This is due to its placement, where the root chakra is much lower, in line with the male sexual organs; and the sacral chakra is higher, in line with women's ovaries.

The energy for this chakra focuses on your relationships, sense of abundance, sexuality, creativity and well-being. This reflects on how you relate with yourself, as well as with others. It also ties in to how your experience with yourself or others leaves you feeling satisfied or dissatisfied. When this chakra is imbalanced, you will experience emotions around jealousy, control, betrayal and power plays. These emotions will limit your ability to progress forward and are likely to eventually cause you mental and physical anguish. This chakra also ties into our connection and ability to accept other people and new experiences.

If you are using this vital energy of this chakra for healing, you should focus on healing uterine problems, impotence, lack of flexibility, lower back pain, sexual difficulties and large intestinal problems. The positioning of this chakra on the lower body is the reason that these are the focus organs or areas.

Healing exercises for this chakra center on the pelvic region. You can opt to execute fairly aggressive exercises or calm movements. Gentle pelvic thrusts and the cobra yoga pose can help you release your vital energy. In addition, it is important to note that this chakra is very dense and physical as well. For this reason, hatha yoga is good. To achieve further healing, especially if you are looking to resolve a sexual issue, you should also attempt a tantric oriented yoga that plays with intimacy issues to stimulate your energy center.

The color of this chakra is orange. Orange is referred to as the color of success and it relates strongly to self-respect. It is the best emotional stimulant, as it connects us to our services and helps remove inhibitions. This makes us independent and highly social. Once we have accomplished these outcomes, then we will be able to experience proper balance to our chakras. However, an imbalance in your chakra could manifest the negative aspects of orange which include being withdrawn, desponded and destructive. This is because when you are unable to interact with people, the temptation is to draw into yourself, and the worst case scenario involves putting yourself down. Finding the balance can be done with inner healing through food that is orange in color like tangerines or oranges.

This chakra is influenced by the emotions that were expressed or repressed in the family as a child. It is at this stage that a child would learn about opposites, the differences between what feels good or bad, and what should be said or kept silent.

Healing also involves more holistic approaches and gemstones for this chakra are Tigers Eye and Orange Calcite. These gemstones can help with centering and drawing focus to the chakra when necessary.

This chakra can also be used for healings of addictions to alcohol, drugs, sex or anything else. In fact, this naval chakra is also known for aiding with solutions related to eating disorders like anorexia nervosa and obesity. It can also help with dealing with past emotions of guilt, anger and shame, keeping you from being judgemental of yourself. If you need a confidence boost, using this chakra will help you say what you mean and mean what you say.

CHAPTER 3 – Solar Plexus Chakra

"Balance between intuition and intellect."

The Sanskrit name for this chakra is *Manipura*.

This is the third chakra in a sequence of seven. The zodiac signs that govern this chakra are Aries, Leo and Sagittarius. These are the signs related to the fire element. If you fall under one of these signs, then this chakra is likely to be the most lively one in your body. From the name Solar, it is safe to say that you should spend some time in sunlight to enjoy all the positive properties of this particular chakra.

This chakra can be found two inches below the breastbone, in the center behind the stomach, below the ribs. It is the center of personal power, passion, ego, anger, impulses and strength. It also centers on psychic development as it is receptive of spirit guides and astral influences. This chakra is where self honouring takes root. When you honour yourself, you are able to see yourself and your actions in a positive light. Ideally, when you partake in any activities that do not bring out the best in you, you should take a moment to stop and get yourself back on track.

A lack of balance in this chakra may lead to lower confidence, confusion, worrying others' opinions about you and depression. There are also physical problems which might manifest including liver issues, food allergies, diabetes and digestive issues. You may also experience some mental or emotional problems when you have a lack of balance with this chakra, including an inferiority complex, and becoming pessimistic and sarcastic. If you have low confidence, you are likely to strongly believe that everyone is better than you, hence the inferiority complex. With pessimism, if you are experiencing feelings of depression for example, you may feel that no matter what you do, you are unable to resolve your situation in any way.

When your solar plexus chakra is balanced, you have feelings of joy and hold yourself in high esteem. You become outgoing and expressive and you have a strong sense of personal power. This makes it easier for you to handle a range of situations and people in a confident way. You are also able to actively think up methods to resolve situations that may arise in this chakra.

The color for this chakra is yellow. As a creative color, yellow is associated with self-worth, governing your feelings about yourselves and how you feel about others' perception of you. Yellow energy connects you to your mental self. With the color of yellow, you can eat foods having this color for healing purposes like corn, chamomile tea, grains and fibre like granola.

The physical health issues that this chakra can be used for include hypoglycemia, diabetes, stomach problems and muscle cramps. The healing exercises you can try include the kundalini yoga pose or on the more active side, a few minutes of vigorous dance. Mentally, this chakra can help you address your issues like fear of change, loss of power, self-respect and so on. For mental healing and balance in your body, you can use visual therapy and yantras which are ideal. As this chakra also deals with self-image, you can speak positive affirmations into your experience.

For a deeper connection, you can use the topaz, yellow calcite or citrine gemstones.

CHAPTER 4 – Heart Chakra

"Healing of spirit, emotions, body and heart take precedence over everything."

In Sanskrit, this chakra is known as *Anahata.*

This is the fourth chakra in a sequence of seven, and it divides the lower chakras from the upper chakras. The zodiac signs that are affected by this chakra are Aquarius, Gemini and Libra. These are all air signs, so this chakra is affected by the air element.

This chakra is so called because of its location which is under the breastbone, in the front and on the spine between the shoulder blades and the back. The center of the heart chakra is love, spirituality and compassion. This chakra directs your ability to love others, to love yourself, to give love and to receive love. It connects with your body and your mind.

The heart chakra is the integration point for all the seven chakras due to a sacred spark of its divine.

If you do not have a healthy heart due to resentment or anger, you need to stop denying your feelings. Allow them to surface so that you can heal and forgive, bringing you closer to yourself.

When this chakra is balanced, your feelings will be empathetic, compassionate and friendly and you will likely see the best in everyone. Picture how you feel when you are in love. Your heart races, you always seem warm all over and you are relaxed and satisfied. However, if your heart is broken for whatever reason, you become an emotional wreck.

Though this may seem to be an emotional problem, it can manifest itself physically through heart attacks, high blood pressure, heart disease and insomnia. When this chakra is out of balance, you will experience paranoia, fear of getting hurt and letting go, indecisiveness, and possible sorry for yourself.

Physically, this chakra rules the heart, shoulders, upper back and circulatory system. Unlike the first three chakras, the heart chakra uses two colors which are pink and/or green. The pink and green chakra relates to your ability to give love and receive it back unconditionally, which is love or self-love.

This chakra is found at the mid-point of the upper chakras and lower chakras. When you need to heal yourself using this chakra, physical contact between people is key.

Giving and receiving love does more than teach us how to nurture ourselves, and it also helps you relax your muscles, thoughts and nerves. As a green chakra balances our energy, we feel renewed harmony and can correct to unconditional love. If it is unbalanced, you will feel indifferent, jealous and bitter.

To take advantage of the electricity in your body, you can use gemstones including Kurzie, Watermelon Tourmaline, Rose Quartz, Jade and Green Aventurine

CHAPTER 5 – Throat Chakra

"New found awareness and direction."

This chakra is known as *Vissudha* in Sanskrit.

This chakra is the fifth in a series of seven. This chakra affects our ability to communicate and it is located in the V of the collarbone at the lower neck. Communication is key to how you interact with yourself, as well as your interaction with the outside world. It captures the possibility of transformation and healing. It is through using your words that you can bring or take away blessings or situations into your life.

This chakra is located in the part of the body where you hold in your anger, and then let it go so that you can experience freedom. The emotional issues it addresses include communication, truth and self-expressed feelings. When there is no balance in these areas, you will feel stifled, and may experience difficulty interacting with others. Unlike the aforementioned chakras, the throat chakra affects no zodiac signs; therefore, it is not affected by any of the elements. Expressing yourself is important and this chakra allows you to speak your peace. If your chakra is balanced, you will speak words that empower you, and if it is imbalanced you say things that disempower you.

Our words are powerful, and what you speak out is a call for manifestation in your life. So, this powerful chakra can be used to control what you want in your life. When your throat chakra is healthy, your voice becomes clear and the truth then resonates. A positive balance in your throat chakra always puts you in a good light. If this chakra and all the energy that it centers around become blocked for any reason, it will be difficult to communicate and you will end up swallowing your emotions. Mentally, this can be potentially poisonous as you begin to harbour negative thoughts that will stop you from communicating. The physical result is a weak voice and confused feelings. This chakra draws its energy between the head and the heart, maintaining integrity between what we think or feel.

If this chakra is out of balance, emotionally you could become timid, quiet, weak and subdued, whereas physically, it will manifest as a sore throat, back pain, hyperthyroid or skin irritations. An unbalanced chakra can create health issues in the throat, ear, voice, esophagus and the throat. If your throat chakra is unbalanced, you will come off as untrustworthy, cold and self-righteous.

There are some healing exercises that you can use for this chakra, and this includes singing a chant, or physically doing a shoulder stand. In fact, this chakra heals and gets balances the best with sound healing. With sound healing, you have the option to send out sound as a mantra type seed sound, chanting or repeating mantras, or in the same way you can take sound in. Each chakra has its own seed sound, which is repeated over and over again to allow mind to clear and the body to relax. The seed sound of this chakra is ham ham ham ham.

For healing meals, you can try fresh fruits, juices and teas.

The main color of the throat chakra is light blue. The color light blue is the color for the spirit and self-expression. Mentally, this is a relaxing color and its effect on the nervous system is pacifying. Blue is also ideal for relaxation, and can help with insomnia.

To reach your energy better, you can use the gemstones of Aquamarine and Azurite.

CHAPTER 6 – Third Eye or Brow Chakra

"Balance the physical and the mental".

The Sanskrit term for this chakra is *Ajna.*

This is the sixth chakra in a series of seven. This chakra can be found above the physical eyes on the middle of your forehead. Its energy focuses on your higher intuition, psychic ability and spirituality. This chakra also helps to eliminate selfish attitudes, while purifying negative tendencies. It also affects your ability to focus on as well as see the bigger picture. It uses your intuition as your guide. When you want to connect with your higher power, the energy from the third eye chakra can also help you receive guidance. When you have a healthy third eye, you are able to perceive every reflection from the outer world. Should this chakra be unbalanced, you will be afraid of success, become egotistical or be non-assertive. The reason that you will become afraid of success is that you will view it as something selfish and undeserved, creating a complex for you where you try as much as possible to underachieve.

Physically, you are likely to experience headaches, blindness, and blurred vision if the chakra is unbalanced. Being conscious of this chakra when it is balanced, you become the master of your destiny, put less stock in material things or you may even experience your past life. On your body, the third eye chakra includes the face, brain, eyes and lymphatic system.

This chakra does not affect any zodiac signs, meaning that this chakra is not affected by any elements.

When you are considering getting help with this chakra, you need to consider various factors. The first one is how much you trust your intuition. If you find that you cannot depend fully on your intuition, then this chakra needs healing. The solution to healing this chakra is visualization. As it governs spirituality, you should allow your imagination to soar and also visualize. If you find yourself constantly justifying your actions, and explaining the reasons for acting without love, then you need to draw on the power of visualization. If you have insight as to what is happening in any situation, then your third eye chakra is close to being balanced. This chakra helps you to see outside the normal realm of your consciousness. And if you need a chakra that will make it easier for you to concentrate, then learning how to perfect the balance of this chakra is what you need to do.

This chakra has the main colors of dark blue. The color dark blue or indigo relates to self responsibility and trusting one's own intuition. Intuition allows you to view things from a spiritual standpoint instead of for satisfaction of your ego or material comfort.

In case your third eye chakras is unbalanced, you will experience negative aspects like being inconsiderate, unable to trust in your intuition, being scatter brained or blurry vision. To resolve these issues, you can try some healing exercises including yoga poses with forward bends or simple exercises. In addition, visualization exercises are particularly effective for healing and balance in this chakra. Foods that are healing for your third eye chakra include chocolate and purple fruits, like grapes and blueberries.

To stimulate healing, you should use the power with gem stones to work with your energy. For this chakra, these gem stones include the Amethyst, Sodalite and Lapis Lazali.

CHAPTER 7 – Crown Chakra

"I and my father are one in complete harmony with my will."

The Sanskrit term for this chakra is *Sahasrara.*

The seventh and final chakra is known as the crown chakra. This energy center can be found just behind the top of the skull. The root chakra which is the first chakra is referred to as the slowest moving chakra. As you climb up to the top, you reach this chakra. The crown chakra, which is known as the chakra, moves with the fastest speed. The crown chakra allows for an incoming flow of wisdom, bringing the gift of cosmic consciousness. It is the energy center for enlightenment, energy and spirituality. Of the seven chakras it is almost entirely spiritual, with no physical attributes that can be referred to. This chakra allows you to connect with God, where life fills your physical body. You can use this chakra to address the following questions: Do you find yourself complaining to God over any unhappiness? Are you inspired a work? Open to new ideas? When you pray to God, do you thank him for all that you are? Through this chakra, you are supposed to be able to reach a higher state of consciousness, allowing for that connection to God to come through clearly. It is believed that through this chakra, you can receive your inspiration from God, allowing you to experience grace as well as a sense of spiritual wellbeing. With these feelings, it becomes simpler to find your ultimate balance and experience true healing, physically and spiritually.

When one discusses the soul and how it comes into your physical body, the crown chakra is suggested to be the entry path at birth. It is suggested that you do not have a soul while in the womb, but you get filled through the crown chakra from the moment you are born. Through your entire life, your soul is able to reside in your body. Your soul then remains in your body until you die, and it is at this point that your soul is supposed to leave your body through the crown to go up to heaven.

This is a particularly sensitive chakra when it comes to imbalance, as it is more spiritual than physical. If this chakra becomes unbalanced, you are likely to experience a feeling of sadness, harbour destructive thoughts or experience frustration. You will feel as though you are losing control and cannot get a grasp back to control. This could result in physical illnesses that include depression, confusion, requests for inspiration and motivation and migraines. If you can master and balance your energy for this chakra, you could open yourself up to the spiritual world, where you can access your subconscious. This will open your entire consciousness to a peaceful experience. Mastering the balance of this chakra can really help you to connect with your higher power.

This chakra deals with the energy around your inner and outer beauty and pure bliss. You can take a two pronged approach to the healing exercises. The first us meditation which focuses on relaxation, resting the mind and ensuring that you are free from intrusive thoughts, or cardio exercises which focuses on stimulation by getting the body active and in that way, sending more blood to the brain to thought consideration.

Rather than healing foods from crown chakra, are benefits from the clean natural world. This means that one can experience healing simply by sitting in the bright sunshine, taking in a deep breath of crisp clean area, or even swimming in the clear blue waters of the bridge.

This chakra is not associated with any zodiac sign and therefore remains unaffected by the four elements of earth, water, fire and air.

The color for the crown chakra is violet. The color violet relates to your self-knowledge and spiritual awareness. It cements the relations between yourself through spirituality and elevated consciousness. You are likely to feel not at ease should there be any imbalance with this chakra. This is because it is mainly spiritual, making it difficult to follow up with any type of physical information. Through this color, you can enhance your creativity and artsy elements. An imbalance can cause feelings of superiority or no contact with reality. In this way, you would revert into your own world, your own consciousness, where you could be the best at everything.

As this chakra is more spiritual than physical, visualization and meditation help you work on your energy. While meditating, you can opt to use seed sounds and gentle noises for meditation purposes. Each chakra has its own sound. For this chakra, the sound is complete silence. The reason for this is because you are meant to end up in a state of pure consciousness.

To connect with your energy with this chakra, you can try Oregon opals, Amethysts and Clear Quartz Crystals. By holding these gemstones near or on your chakra area, you are able to transfer energy from your body to the stone.

CHAPTER 8- Chakra and Meditation

"No Man is free who is not a master of himself"- Epictetus

In order to attain the best results while trying to get in touch with the 7 energy levels, it is vital to consider incorporating various aspects of meditation. That is why this chapter is dedicated to understanding what meditation is, in relation to chakra.

Meditation, in general, is the exercise that brings the self to a state of being in the moment, in which one is fully aware of what is happening around them at the moment. However, some people have mistakenly understood meditation as the ability to fully concentrate on a specific thing.

While this is one of the many aspects of meditation, it does not fully reach the depths of meditation, nor bring out the goals of the practice. When you try to concentrate on a particular thing, you tend to think deeply about it, ignoring everything else around. Experts in the field will tell you that this can be frustrating, especially because it is normally a very hard thing to do to stop the mind all together or to stop it from what it is used to doing.

Other schools of thought have it that meditation calls for taking time off everything and having a quiet secluded moment in which you ponder, in an effort to attain peace and calmness. However, many people still lack knowledge on the how aspect of meditation and some people give up on it altogether, not realizing that is does not have to be a complicated procedure or exercise. It would at this point be prudent to point out what meditation is not, for purposes of bringing the beginner to the same level as the expert in the field.

Meditation is not concentration – Meditation does not try to fix the mind on a particular object like it happens in concentration.

Meditation is not loss of control – while meditating, blocking movements, sounds, colors or voices around you is uncalled for. It only results to loss of control and one becomes less aware of what is around them, which is not a motive of meditation.

Meditation is not exercises of breathing and maintaining a given posture. This may constitute one of the steps to attaining the highest level of meditation if under the guidance of a master in the practice, but in isolation they do not equal meditation.

Meditation is not mental effort – you do not have to force your mind to attain a given mental status.

Meditation hence places emphasis on being fully aware of the thoughts that come to mind and not try to stop them or even categorize them as right or wrong. As some people say, you can meditate while doing just about anything, but for the purposes of understanding the importance of meditation to chakras, we will go a step further and discuss how to get it right further in the chapters.

So, how do meditation and chakra complement each other? According to the research that has been done over the years concerning meditation, the practice has the greatest potential of reducing stress, much more effectively than other stress-reduction strategies that have been proposed in the past. Stress reduces energy levels in very many significant parts of the body, soul and mind. Through meditation, one is able to regain these lost energy levels, or in other words, get in touch with the seven energy centers (chakras), one at a time.

In every person there is a body of energy levels known as nadis, which are distributed in the seven energy centers (chakras). Beneath these two systems is a dormant energy (kundalini) that nurtures and protects the human being and once it awakened, it travels through the spine, through each of the chakras and finds its way out through the top area of head at the fontanelle bone. The energy can be felt on the palms and on top of the head. In case of any imbalance in the kundalini, the impact is felt on the hands. This process is what is known in many circles as self-realization of enlightenment. By mastering this art, one is able to decode the state of the kundalini, hence releasing energy to the chakras.

The subtle body emits the following seven emotions: integration, forgiveness, equality, security, peace, creativity and innocence, which represent the seven chakras from the seventh to the first one respectively. By being able to balance these emotions, the qualities within an individual are awakened and enhanced, hence bringing balance and an enhanced level of integration. This is the result of peace and joy. Before the kundalini subtle system is awakened, the chakras are prone to exhaustion and they are limited in energy levels. Once they come into contact with kundalini, they attain the infinite level of super consciousness in which there is the divine power of love.

Kundalini has three energy levels, each of which is significant and responsible for given emotions and habits. The first level is the left channel, also known as the ida nadi. The dominant color for this channel is blue and the symbolic meaning is that it corresponds and connects you to your emotions, past, affectivity and desires. At its highest level, it connects to the superego, which designs the conditionings, memories and habits that you frequently bring out.

The other channel is the right channel which is also known as pingala nadi. It is represented by the color yellow and the functions of this channel are planning and activity, both mental and physical. It is the channel that gives meaning and puts more sense to the ego, the aspect which separates an individual from the rest of the world.

The third channel is the central channel, which is called the sushumna nadi. It is the channel that carries the power to sustain evolution and which also guides the conscious and unconscious parts of the brain towards a higher level of awareness at the sahasrara, which is the seventh chakra.

CHAPTER 9- How to Open your Spiritual Chakras

"They are the weakest, however strong, who have no faith in themselves or their own powers."- Christian Bovee

There are many teachings on the spiritual inner being, and according to Hindu/Buddhism teachings, the chakras are very vital in the general wellness of a human being. It is through the chakras that feelings and thinking come together, and while some chakras are not all active, some are over-active and if one does not achieve a state of balance between the two, it becomes nearly impossible to attain a state of peace.

Step 1

In the previous chapter, we looked at meditation in relation to chakras. How then do you open up to your spiritual chakras through meditation? The first and foremost thing that you need to know is that you do not need to make the over-active chakras less active. Just like in meditation, you do not have to overwork the mind faculty in an effort to attain a desired state of mind of level of energy. The over-active chakras simply compensate for the inactive or the less open ones, and this way, they complement each other. With time, the less active chakras open up and the energies become evenly distributed, hence balancing the system.

Step 2

Once this is clear, the next step entails opening the root chakra which is represented by color red. This is the chakra that is convened with the ability to become fully aware of your surroundings and being comfortable in different situations. Once you have fully connected to this level, the feeling that results is a feeling of balance, stability, security and everything around you makes sense. While you are in this level, you have no reason or are never tempted to distrust people for no apparent reason. This is the level in which you are able to control your body between fear and over-confidence, greed and moderation, insecurity and security. At this point you are welcome to any change that may be necessary to your well-being.

There are specific activities that you may want to engage in at this point like yoga, walking or manual house work which will go a long way in strengthening the chakra. While you do any of these activities, ensure that your feet remain grounded such that you can feel the ground beneath you. For best results, stand up relaxed in a straight posture then slightly part the feet and bend the knees a little. Slightly move the pelvis forward, making sure to keep the body balanced, then sink your weight forward with your weight evenly distributed, maintain the posture for several minutes.

Change position and sit down with your legs crossed, placing your wrists on your knees and bringing your thumb and index finger of each hand to touch, in a gentle, peaceful manner. You may close your eyes and bring your mind to focus on the root chakra and its full meaning, which represents the spot between the genitals and the anus. Ensure that you chant the sound LAM clearly but silently while maintaining a relaxed mode. Let your mind explore the meaning of the chakra and how it affects your life in general. There is no fixed rule as to how long you should continue with this meditation, but it is recommendable that you do it until you are relaxed completely and you attain a feeling of having a 'clean' system in the inside of you. Picture a red closed flower and imagine that some energy is radiating it, making it slowly open and display its four fully energized petals. Contract the pelvic area and gently relax it as you breathe in and out slowly.

Step 3

The third step is open the Sacral Chakra whose color of representation is orange. This is the energy center that is concerned with sexuality and feelings. If you are able to fully open up the center, you reach a point where feelings are released with liberty and without the risk of becoming over-emotional. You also become outgoing, passionate and are open to affinity and problems based on sexuality are nothing that you cannot solve. Take note that if this chakra is not active enough, the resultant condition is impassivity and lack of emotional feelings, which leads you to close up to yourself and fail to open to anyone. On the other hand, if the chakra is over-stimulated and becomes over-active, the resultant condition is that you will be very emotional, sexual and sensitive even to very small matters.

To attain the idea level of this chakra through meditation, observe the steps outlined below:

- Kneel down then sit on your knees, making sure that your back is not curved and that it is also relaxed.

- Place your hands on your laps, with the palms facing upwards, one on top of the other, precisely with the right palm on top of the left one, with the thumbs touching softly.

- Bring your mind to meditate about the Sacral Chakra, which is basically about the lower back.

- As you meditate, softly but clearly chant the work VAM, letting yourself sit still and relaxed until you get to the point where you feel relaxed and your feelings are 'clean.'

Step 4

This entails opening the navel chakra whose color is yellow and is responsible for your confidence, especially when you find yourself in a group. If you successfully open this energy center, you will be rewarded with a feeling of being in control and having dignity in yourself. If it does not open up or does not attain an active status, the result is that you will feel indecisive and passive. This leads you to being apprehensive most of the time. However, if the chakra is over-active, you will have to contend with aggression and arrogance.

To open the chakra through meditation:

- Sit on your knees with your back straight and relax.

- Place your hands just beneath your stomach at the solar plexus and bring the tips of both hands to touch as they point away from your body. Let the thumbs cross while the fingers remain in straight. Attach importance to this as it is a meditation procedure that helps you attain the level of cleanliness in the system that you desire.

- Bring your mind to concentrate on this chakra, its meaning as far as the spine above the navel is concerned and how it affects your life.

- The sound to chant at this level is "RAM".

- As the previous chakras, ensure that you continue with the meditation until you attain a state of calmness and relaxation.

Step 5

The next chakra to open up is the heart chakra which is represented by the color green. Its concentration is mainly on the heart, and the virtues that come out of it include endearment, care and love. By attaining a level of openness in this chakra, you will become compassionate, amicable in relationships and friendly to all. When the chakra is not active, an individual becomes cold and unfriendly towards other people and when it is over-active, your love and friendliness to people often chokes them without you realizing it. Unfortunately, people tend to interpret this as selfishness.

Meditation steps for heart chakra

- Sit on the floor with your legs crossed and bring the tips of your fingers and thumbs on both hands to touch each other.

- Place the left hand on the left knee with the palm facing upwards. The right hand should be placed on the center of the chest, with the index finger and thumb touching at the tip.

- As with the other chakras, concentrate on the meaning of the heart chakra at its level with the heart and spine.

- The sounds to chant at this level are "YAM" and again ensure that you do it silently but clearly.

- Meditate until you attain a level of clarity.

Step 6

This is about the throat chakra whose color is light blue. The chakra's focus in on the ability to express yourself and communicate clearly in front of people, be it a small or a big group. When you are in touch with the chakra, you are able to easily express yourself, especially through art. When the chakra is not activated, one tends not to talk a lot and you make come out as shy. This is the chakra that needs to be deactivated if one finds himself constantly telling lies. When the chakra is in an overactive state, the result is that an individual tends to talk too much and this annoys people. Listening to other people also becomes a big challenge because you cannot bring yourself to that level.

The meditation posture and procedure for the throat chakra is as follows:

- Sitting on your knees with your back straight and relaxed, cross your fingers on both hands, with the thumbs touching at the top, as they touch the base of the throat.

- Meditate on the meaning of the throat chakra and how it represents aspects of your life and affects it.

- The sound to chant at this level is "HAM".

- Relax the body while thinking of the chakra until you attain the desired level of relation and clarity.

Step 7

This is the level at which you get in touch with the Third Eye Chakra whose color is blue. Just like its name suggest, the chakra is concerned with issues of insight. When it is open a person tends to have many dreams and excellent clairvoyance, but when it is not, the ability to think for oneself is undermined. When the chakra is over-active, daydreaming becomes the order of the day. In the extreme, a person may suffer from continued and prolonged hallucinations.

For meditation posture:

- Sit on a flat stable surface with the legs crossed and place your hands on the lower part of the chest, with the middle fingers touching each other at the top and facing away from the body. The other fingers should bend at touch the upper phalanges. The thumbs should point towards the body and touch at the top.

- Meditate on the throat chakra as you chant the sound "OM" while feeling the body relax with ease. Find meaning for the chakra and how it affects your life.

Step 8

You have finally reached the highest level of energy and you now want to open the crown chakra. This is the most spiritual chakra because it has to do with wisdom and how one relates with the universe. When the chakra is in operation, an individual is less prejudice and becomes more aware of what is around them. It is the level at which you are able to connect with yourself and enjoy each moment of life as it comes. If the chakra is not active, a person becomes very rigid in their thought process and spirituality lacks place in your being. When the chakra is overactive, the result is that you tend to look at everything intellectually or spiritually at all time. Such people may at such times forget about their most basic needs like food and water.

Posture:

- Sit down on a flat surface with your legs crossed and place your hands before the stomach, with both the little fingers pointing upwards and away from the body. The rest of the fingers should cross, with the left thumb under the right one.

- Bring your mind to think about the crown chakra, its meaning and significance.

- The sound for this stage is "NG" as hard as it may sound. This is because those who attain this level of meditation are those that have fully subjected their bodies and mind to this powerful exercise.

- Please note that this is the longest meditation step as it takes more than ten minutes and it should not be used if the very first chakra or level of meditation is not based on a strong foundation. Remember that the energy will be leaving the body through the top most part of the body. If the root chakra is not strong enough, you may lose yourself in the process.

CHAPTER 10- Meditation Tips For Beginners: How to Make Meditation Work in Chakras

"What we feel and think and are is to a great extent determined by the state of our ductless glands and viscera."- Aldous Huxley

Even though I have pointed out how to meditate and attain the best results for each chakra, it is worth noting that meditation is not as easy as it appears to be in writing, especially so if you are a beginner and have no master to guide you through the process. It, therefore, goes without saying that the temptation to give up along the way is usually high. However, the result of perseverance is a bunch of rewards that you will never get 0over in the course of your life. Practice and perseverance will help you achieve that state of peaceful living, if only you will add patience to it.

This chapter is dedicated to beginners who want to open up the seven chakras through meditation, but have no idea where to start of how to maintain the meditation practice on a daily basis.

Tip 1

Come up with a regular schedule during which you practice meditation. When you attach importance to your meditation practice, it will go without saying that you will give it all the time it needs for you to get in touch with yourself. Since you cannot meditate the whole day and neglect other aspects of your life, you will do all you can to see to it that you set aside at least 15 minutes of your time, especially in the morning when your mind is still fresh. When you think of how easy it usually is for anyone to waste 15 minutes gossiping, chatting or doing nothing really important, you will see just how easy it is to save those 15 minutes by actually investing them in the betterment of your life.

Tip 2

Always strive to begin your day with meditation no matter how short the session. Meditation helps you attain a state of peace and calmness and this moment of silence can see your day move from bad to good. The earlier in the morning that you do this, the easier it will be for you to feel the vibration and thoughtlessness at the present moment. Most chakras usually open up during morning meditation.

Tip 3

This works hand in hand with tip 2 above, and it is all about letting yourself relax and open up during meditation. Allow your energy systems to communicate to each other and to your body organs as well. Allow energy to pass through the organs freely, and more importantly, give and receive energy to and from your surroundings.

Tip 4

Remember that the meditation techniques outlined previously may not work effectively if you harbour un-forgiveness within you. If thoughts that offend you come to mind, just say out silently but clearly "I forgive, I forgive, and I forgive." This has the effect of making the kundalini take the negative thoughts away from you. Forgiveness is the key to being aware of the present moment.

Tip 5

Make use of meditation candles and music. They will help you focus and draw your attention to what needs to be done at the moment. They also help you connect with other meditators who are at a higher and more advanced level of meditation. In connection to this, always learn to let go of the need to control your thoughts, your focus or your imagination, just let your mind relax and allow thoughts to come and leave at their own pleasure.

Tip 6

For your evening meditation, strive to soak your feet in warm water before you embark on the exercise. You will not only have better meditation sessions, but you will also sleep better than on the nights when you do not meditate. You also will wake up better refreshed and energized.

Tip 7

Get in touch with your kundalini as you meditate, and speak with it. Remember that meditation does not have to be a morning or evening only ritual, but can be done at any time of the day. Having inner communication with kundalini whether you are driving or working on your computer will help you get to a state of thoughtless awareness. When you ask her for spiritual balance or evolution, she will rise within you and help you rise beyond yourself and connect with the universe.

As a secondary tip to this one, once you have made your desires known to kundalini, let her do the rest of the work for you. In other words, always leave your worries, anxieties and doubts with this energy source. Once you surrender to her, she will be faithful enough to clear out all your problems on your behalf. For this to be more effective, say the words out loud. For example you could say "I leave all my problems to you Kundalini, I leave all my cares to you."

Tip 8

Meditation calls for the use of your sixth sense which, in the context of chakra, is the Sahasrara or the limbic area. Throughout the day, ensure that you are consciously aware of the vibrations that happen above your head, and see to it that your intentions become clear beyond the mind level, and into the sahasrara. Let this be the area from which you precept anything you hear or see.

Tip 9

Do not think about anything. Visualize your thoughts like airplanes which land and take off at an airport. They just come and go, and this is what should be happening with your thoughts. Do not attempt to analyze or even think why you got the thought in the first place. Just be aware that the thoughts are there and do not try to stope them either.

Tip 10

Doing it with others makes you grow faster and remain at it for longer. When everyone lights their candle, there is more light, and collective meditation causes a stronger flow of vibrations, which it turn give rise to more pure and divine energy. The Kundalini works better and more effectively when it is awakened in the presence of other practitioners. You also get to learn new meditation techniques that you knew nothing about.

Conclusion

Once you understand your chakras, you can enter a new level of consciousness, as well as increase your health by leaps and bounds. Then, when you begin to get the delicate balances just right, you will find yourself able to maintain the benefits you can get, as well as incorporate using chakras in your everyday life.

Chakras are about energy, and the seven chakras discussed in this book focus on aspects of your body for your spiritual and physical health. To bring about healing and balance, the methods that they employ include:

- Yoga – A variety of yoga styles can be used as chakra healing exercises. These are meant to bring you closer to your chosen energy center, for reasons including healing, relaxation or stimulation.
- Meditation – This is ideal for the chakras that focus more on the mind than on the body. Meditation allows you to get closer to yourself and your higher being, magnifying the achievements and positivity of a chakra.
- Physical Exercise – Whether it is walking, dancing or running like the wing, the aspect of physical exercise and its uses come up in several of the chakras. Exercise allows blood to flow throughout the body allowing for alertness.

In addition to these healing methods, you can take advantage of gem stones for your focused energy center so that they can elevate that energy, which in turn can help you achieve a predetermined goal.

Finally, if you are starting out with understanding chakras and their effects, evaluate your zodiac sign and see whether it matches your description with the chakras. This will give you an idea of where to focus your energy and should lead you to becoming peaceful, and striking a balance with your emotional, physical and mental needs.

Printed in Great Britain
by Amazon.co.uk, Ltd.,
Marston Gate.